Dear color enthusiasts,

dive into the vibrant and picturesque world of Italy with our enchanting Summer Scenes Coloring Book. Immerse yourself in 20 beautifully hand-drawn illustrations capturing the essence of Italian summer.

Authentic Italian Charm
Diverse Landscapes
Cultural Delights
Lively Activities
Charming Details
Relaxing and Inspiring

Experiment with Materials: Use crayons, colored pencils, and markers to create different effects. Mix and match materials to achieve a range of colors and textures.

Color Shades: Experiment with color shades and gradients to add depth and movement to your illustrations. Don't be afraid to be bold!

Your Magical Tools:

Crayons: For bold and vibrant colors.

Colored Pencils: For precise details and gradual shading.

Markers: For intense colors and a variety of lines.

Remember: This coloring book is an invitation to have fun. There are no strict rules, just space to express your unique vision. Let yourself be inspired by the beauty of vintage pick-up trucks and transform each page into a unique masterpiece. Happy journey into the world of color!

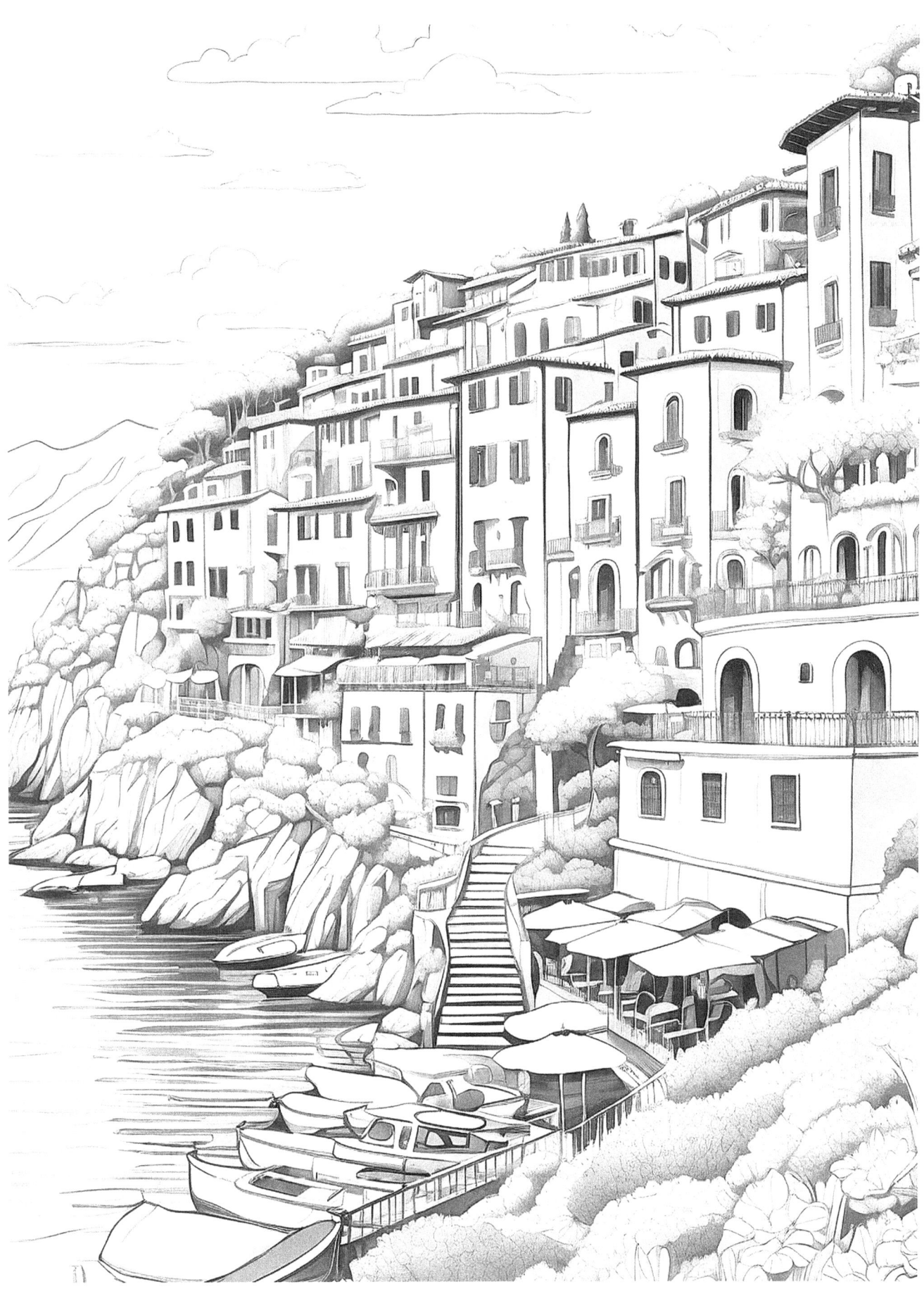

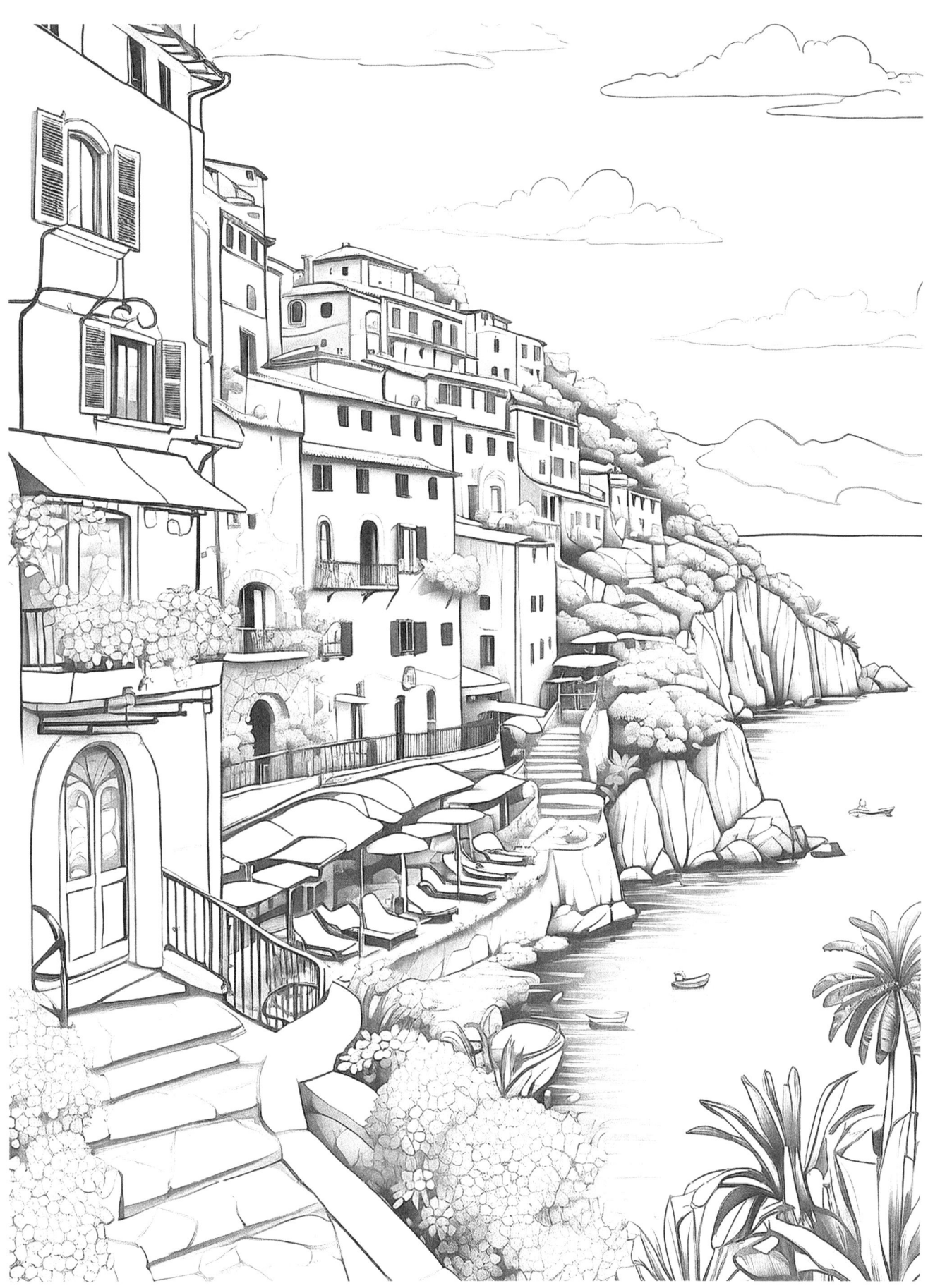

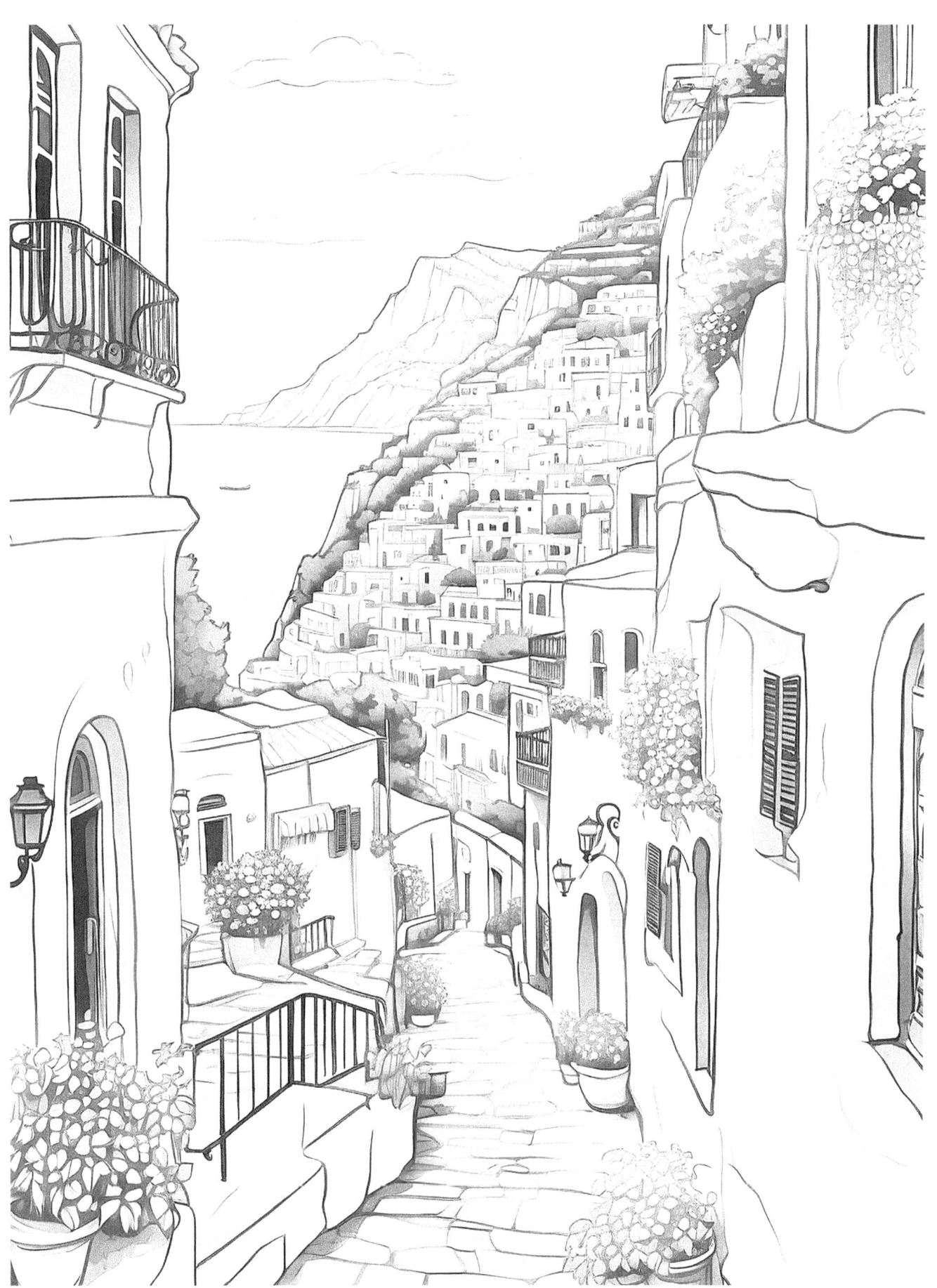

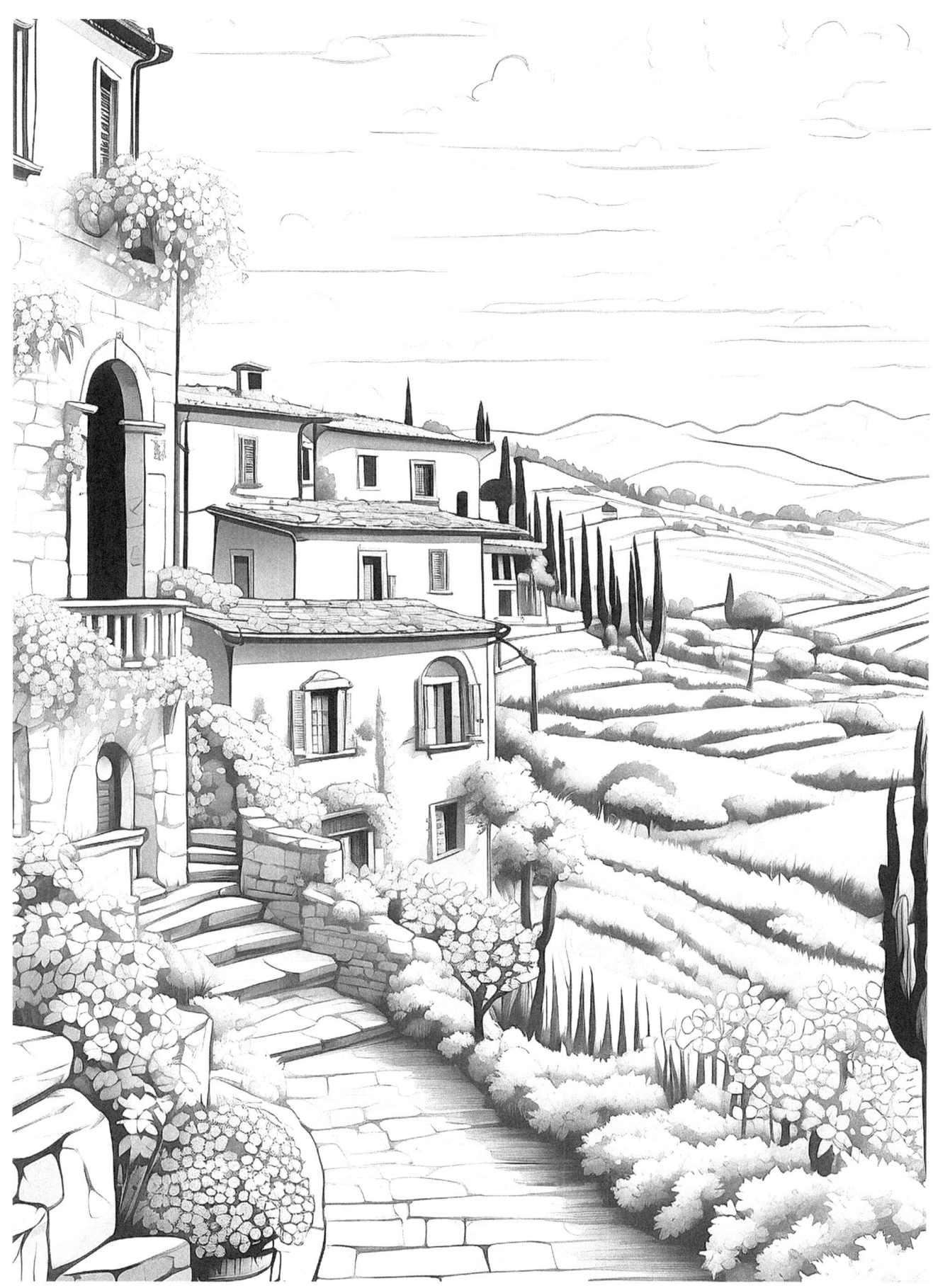

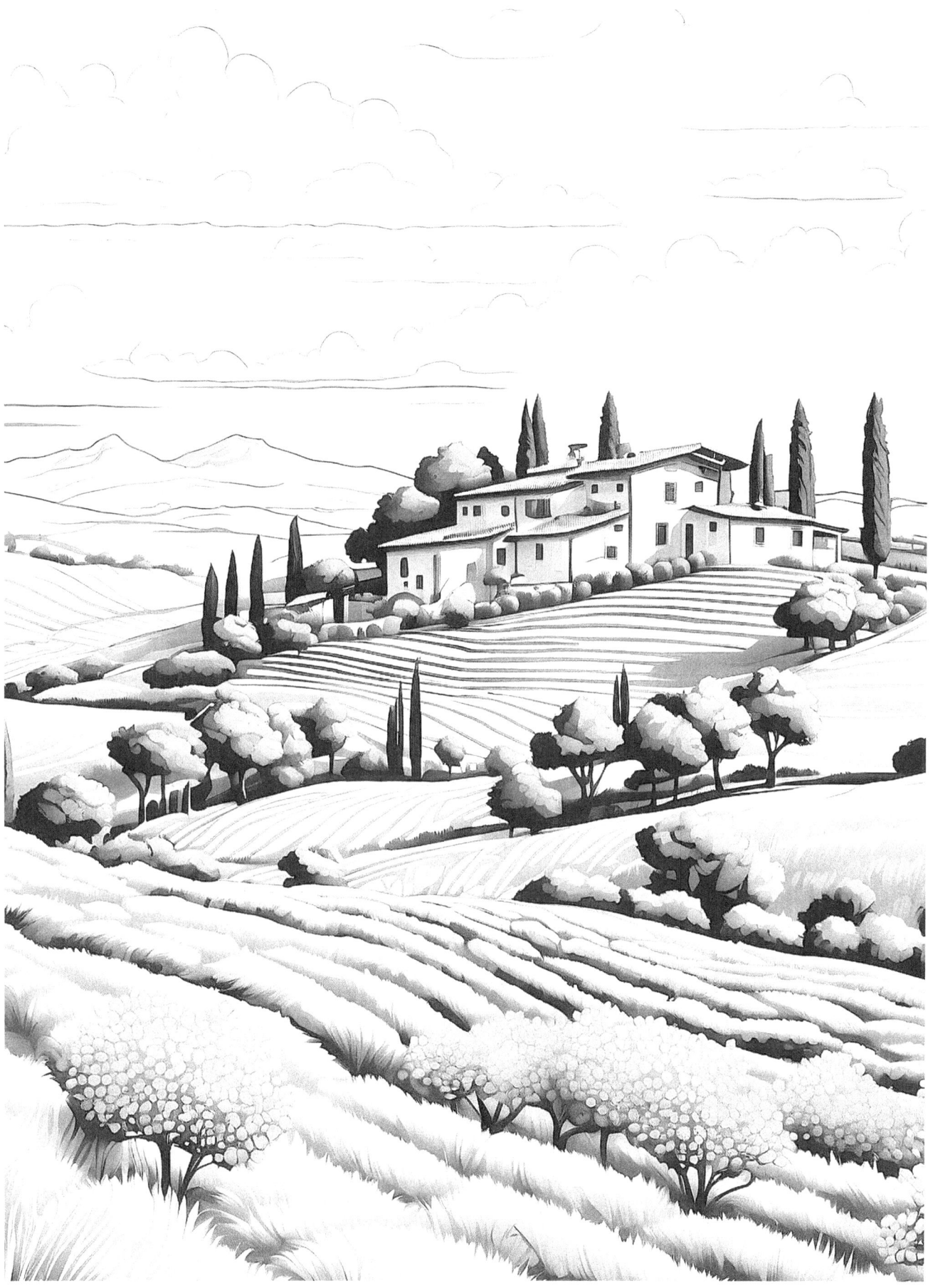

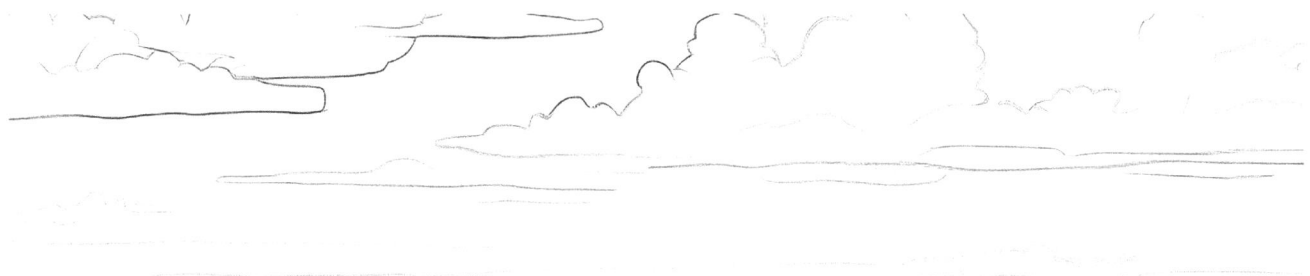

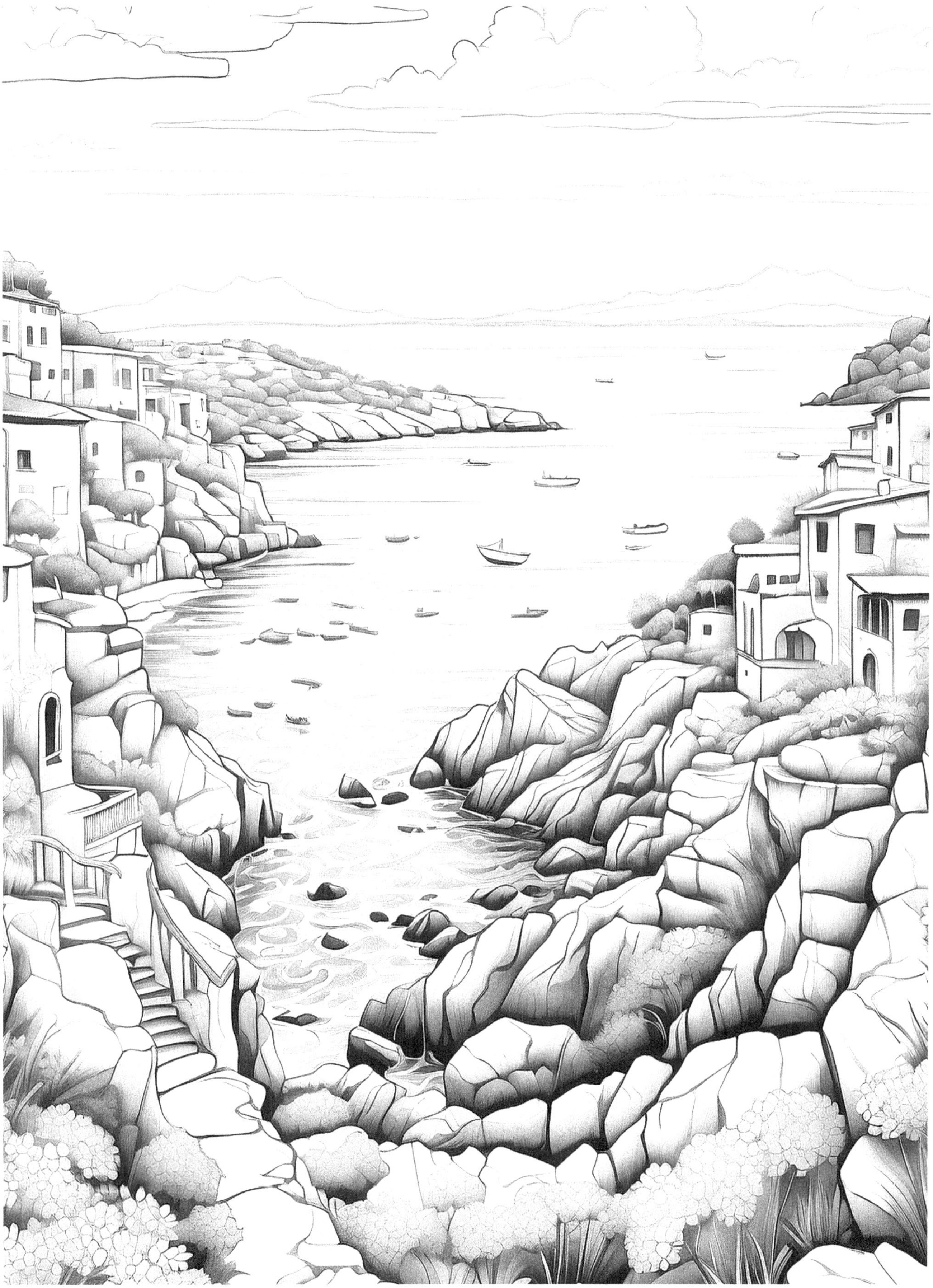

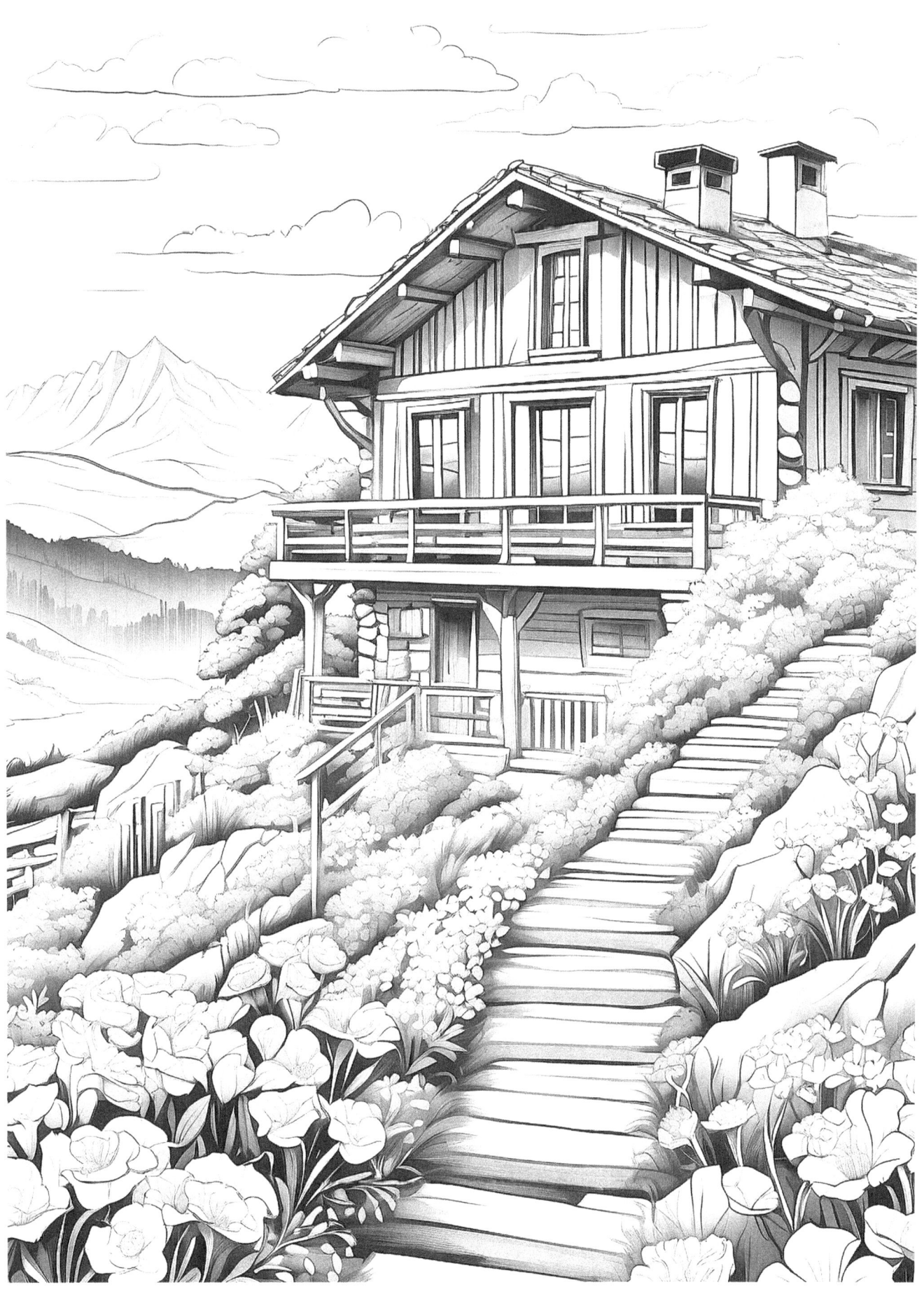

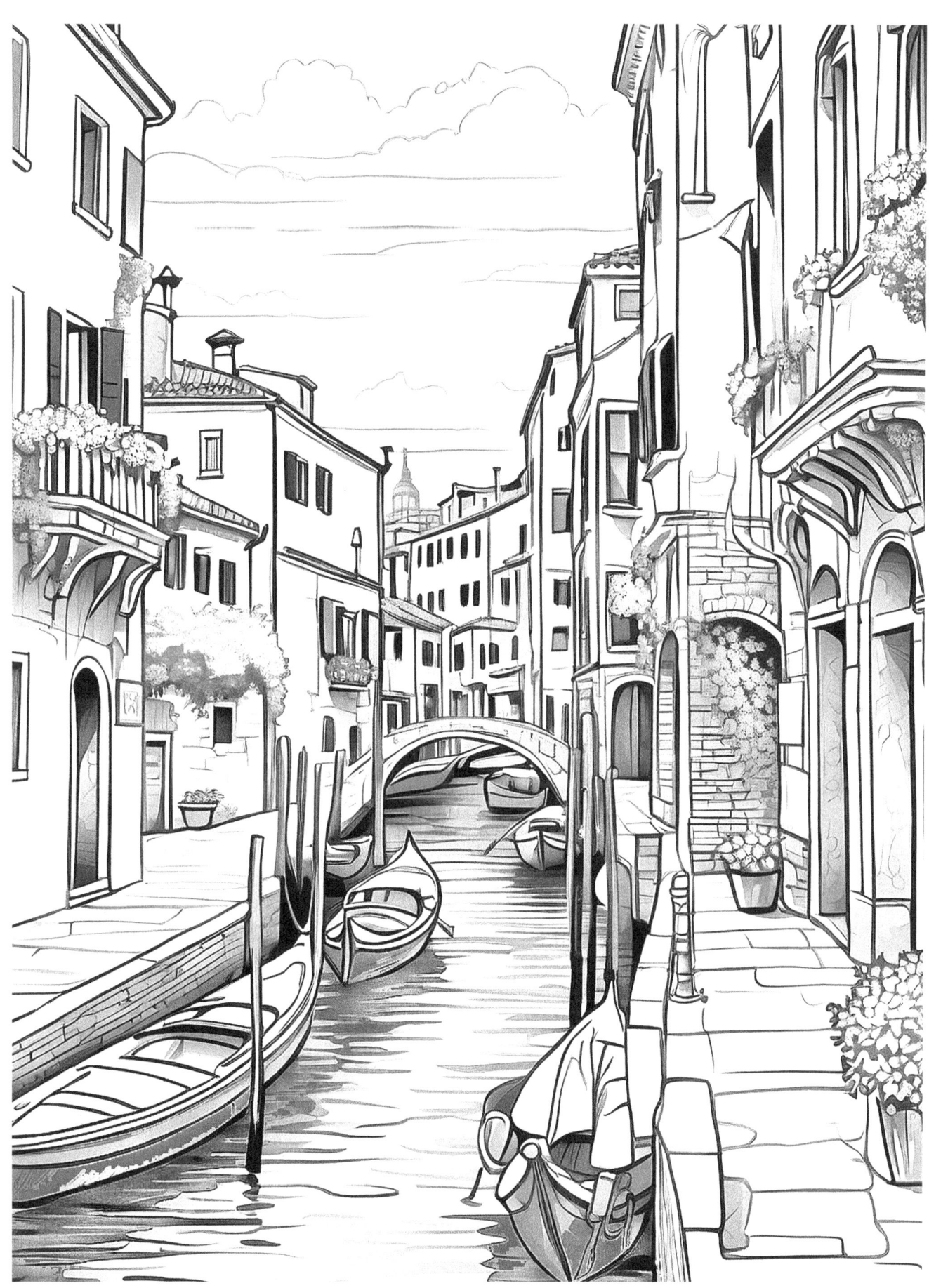

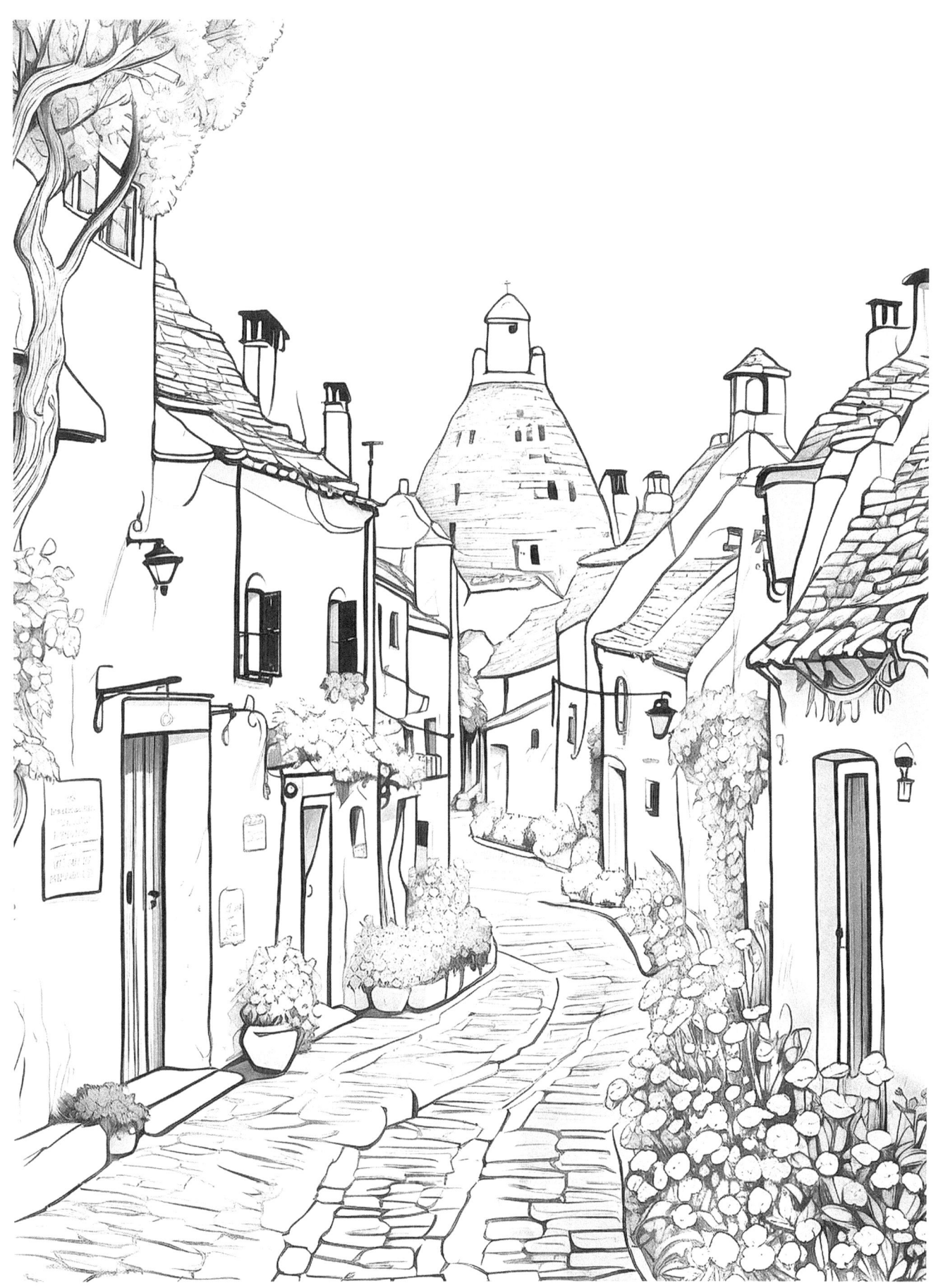

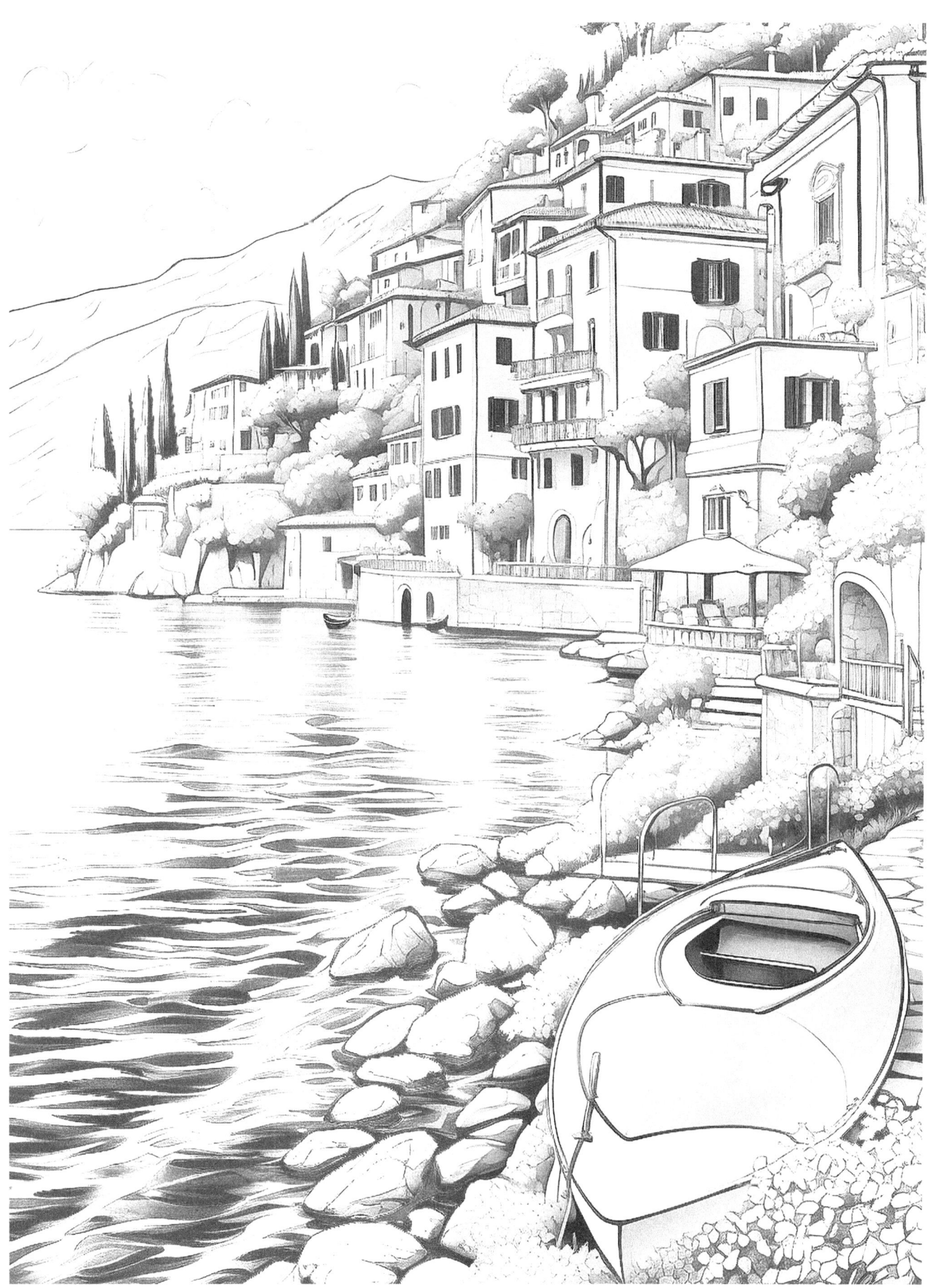

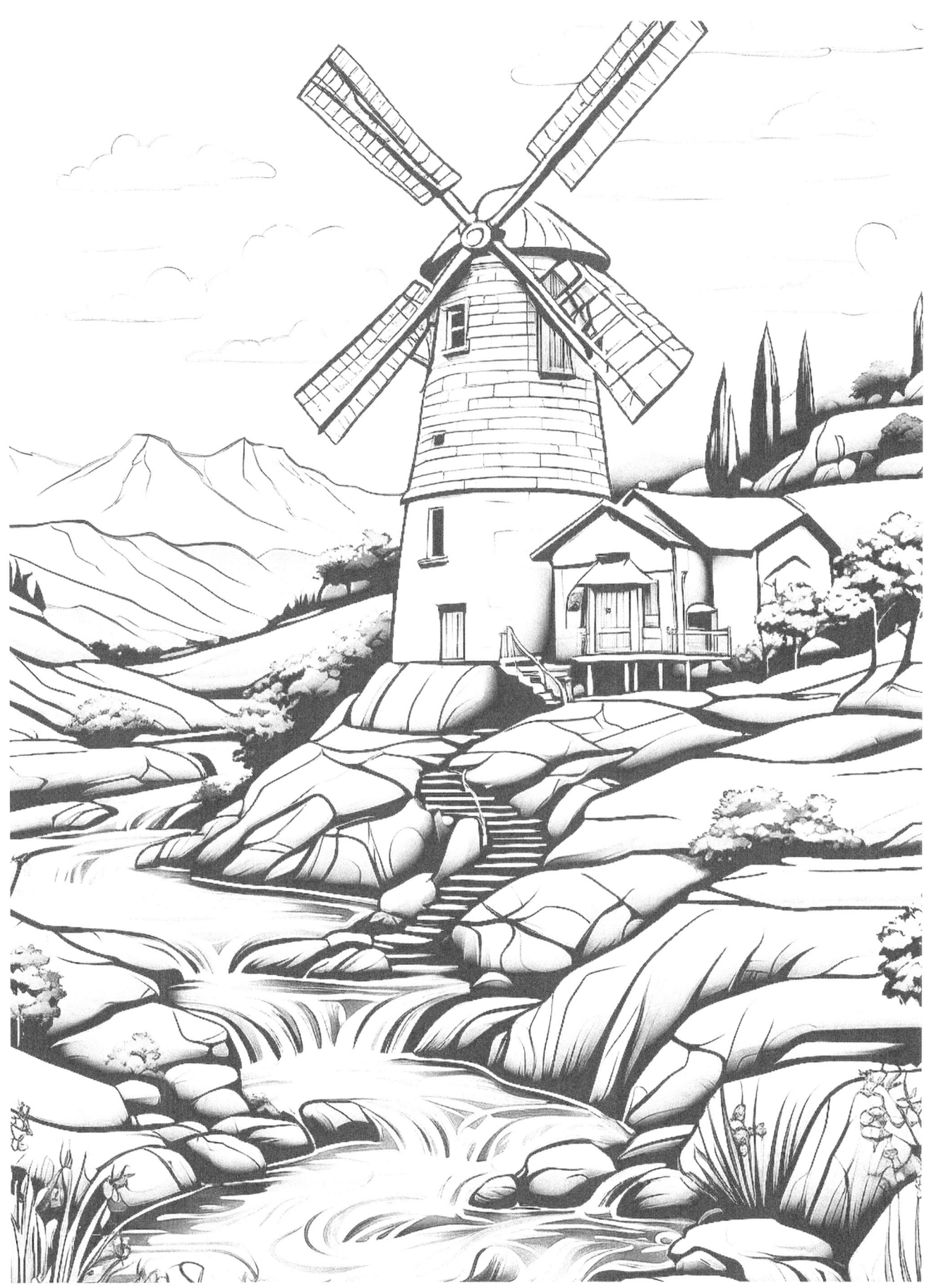

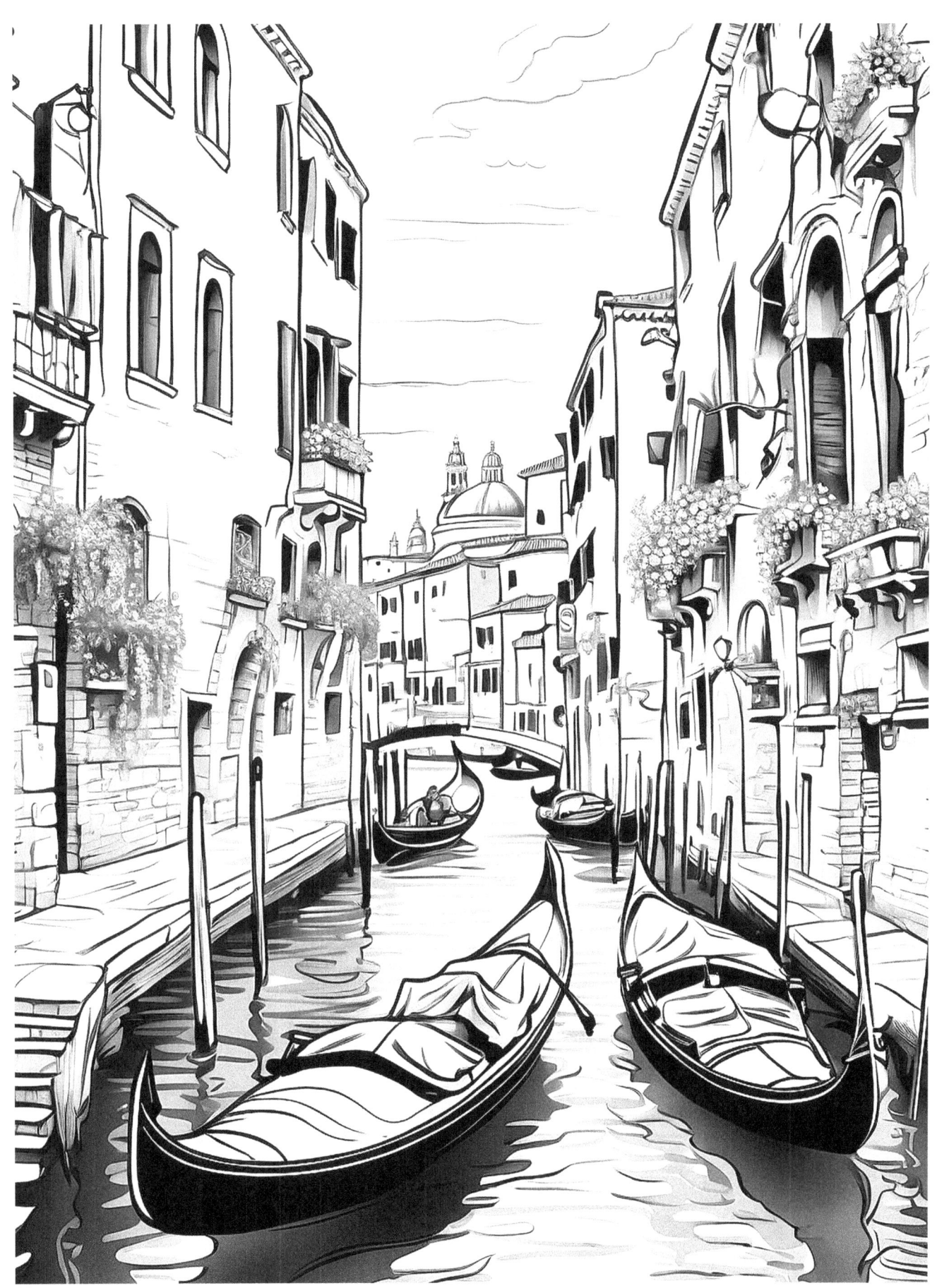

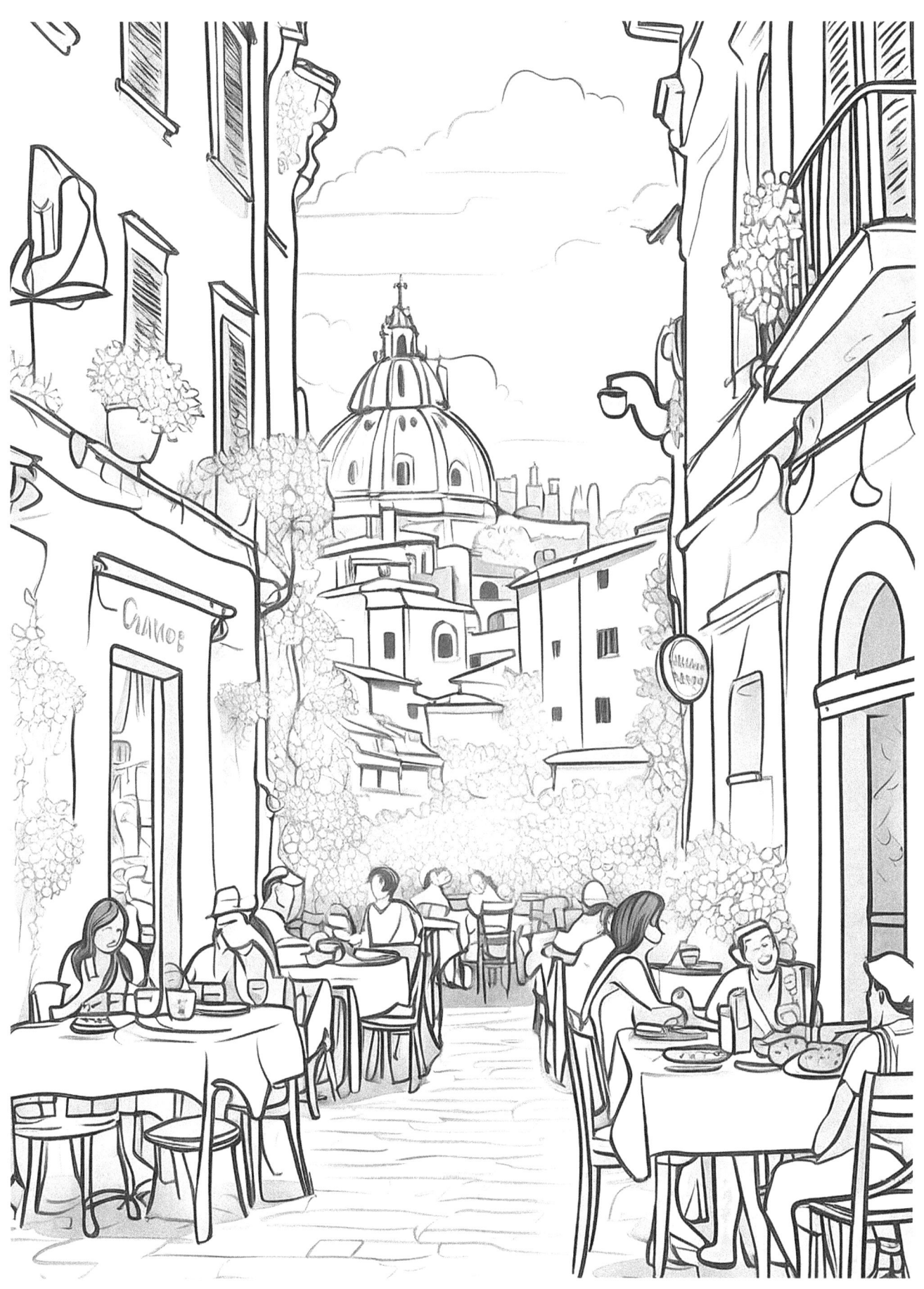

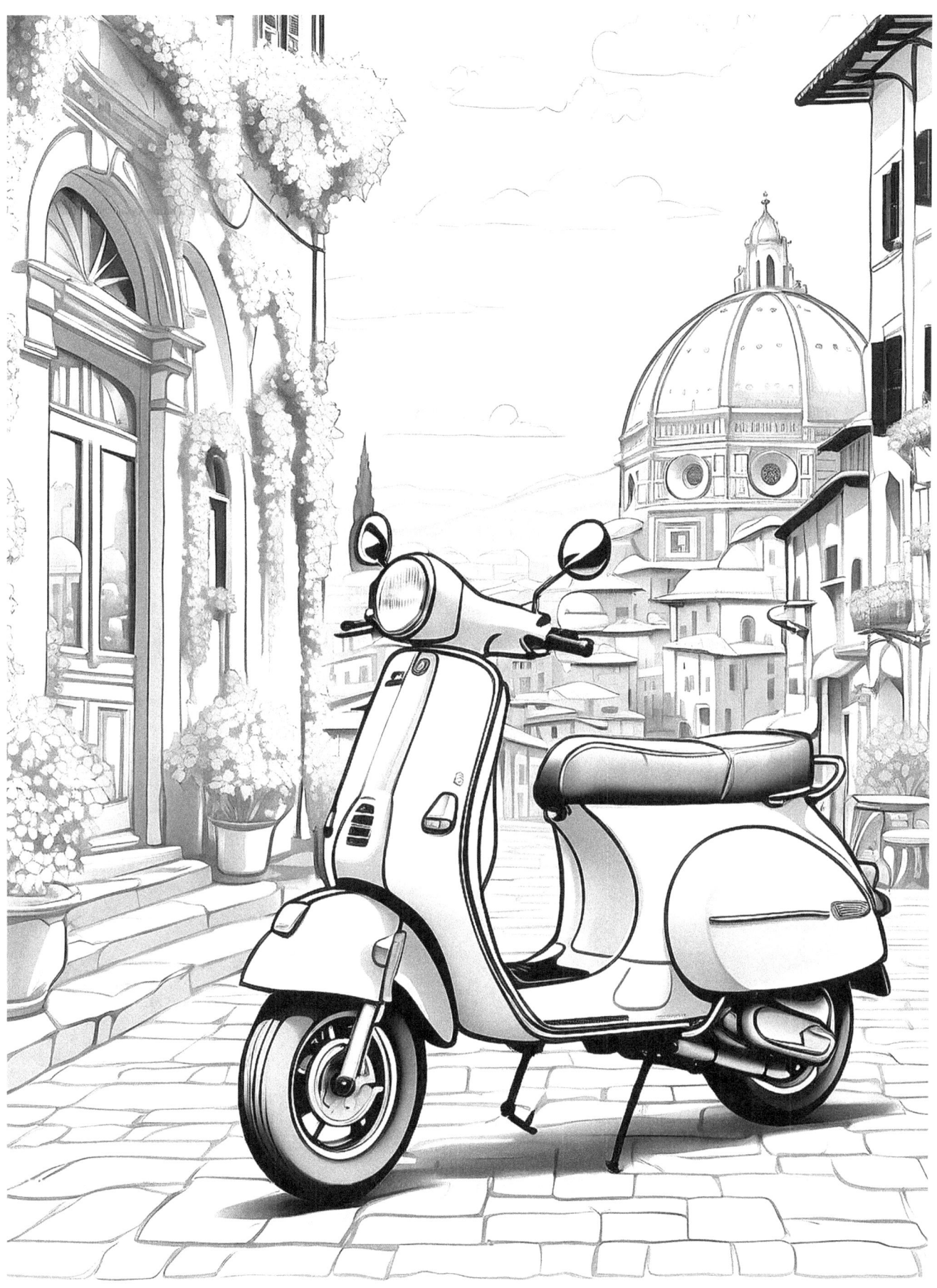

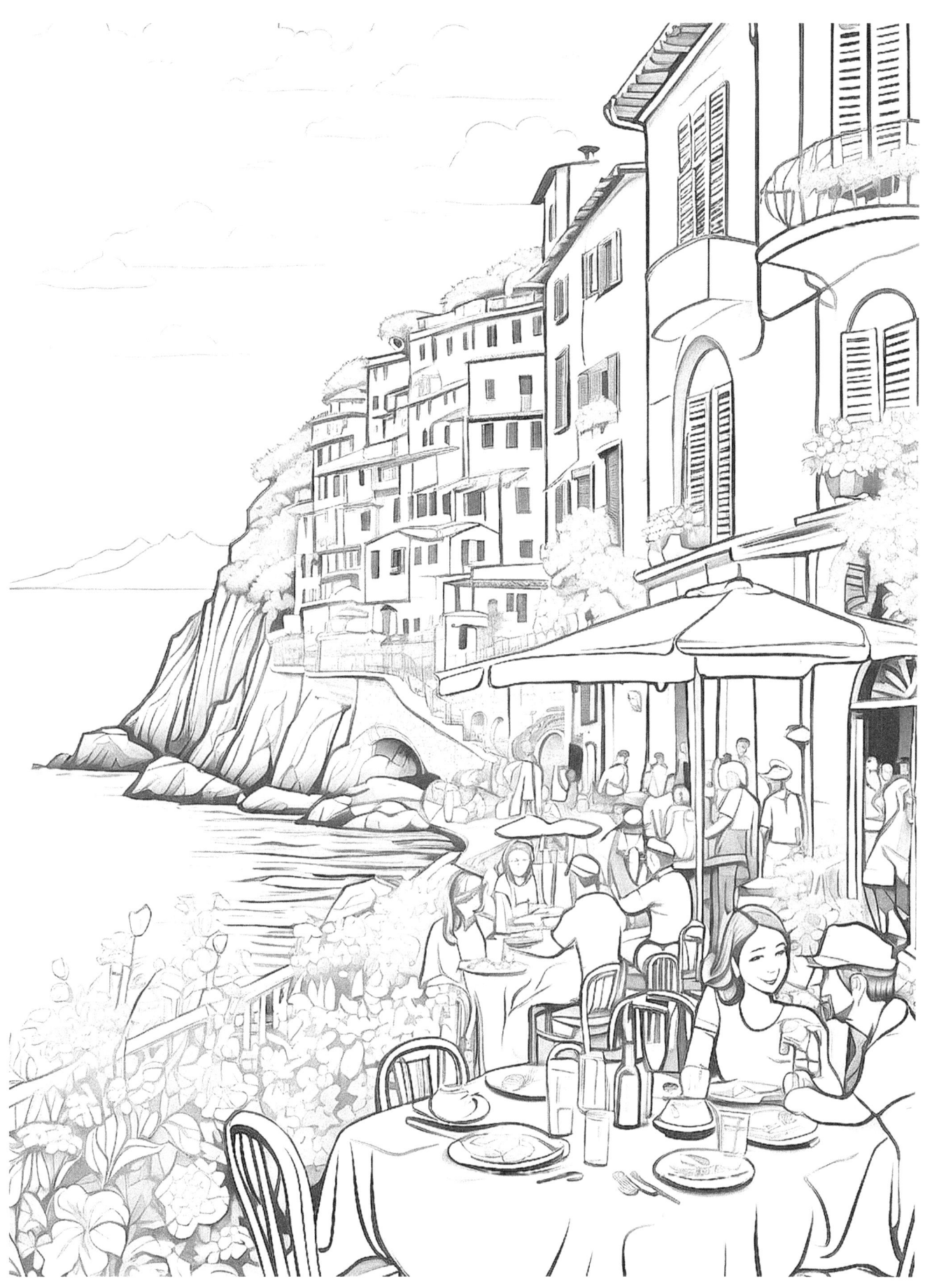

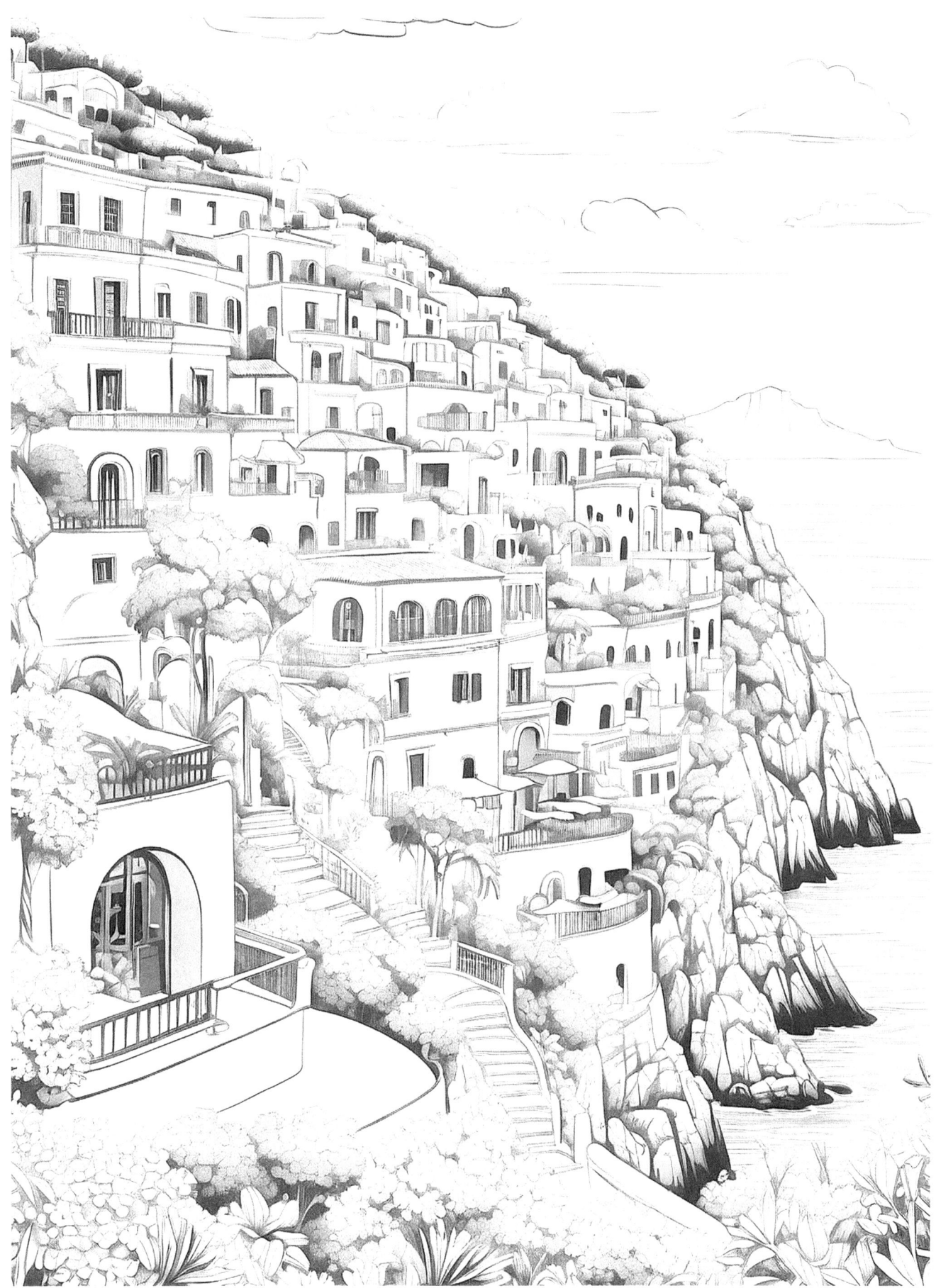

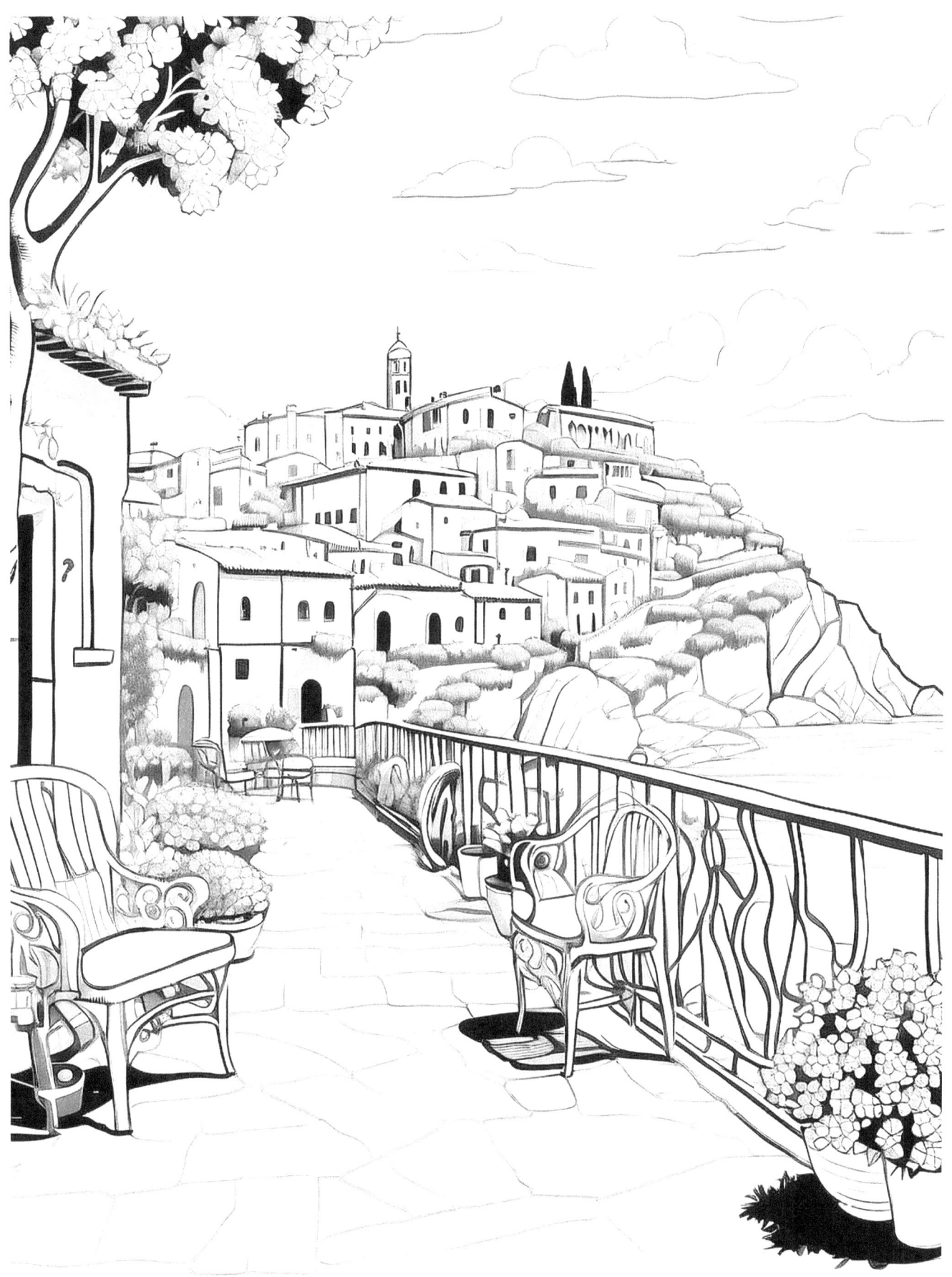

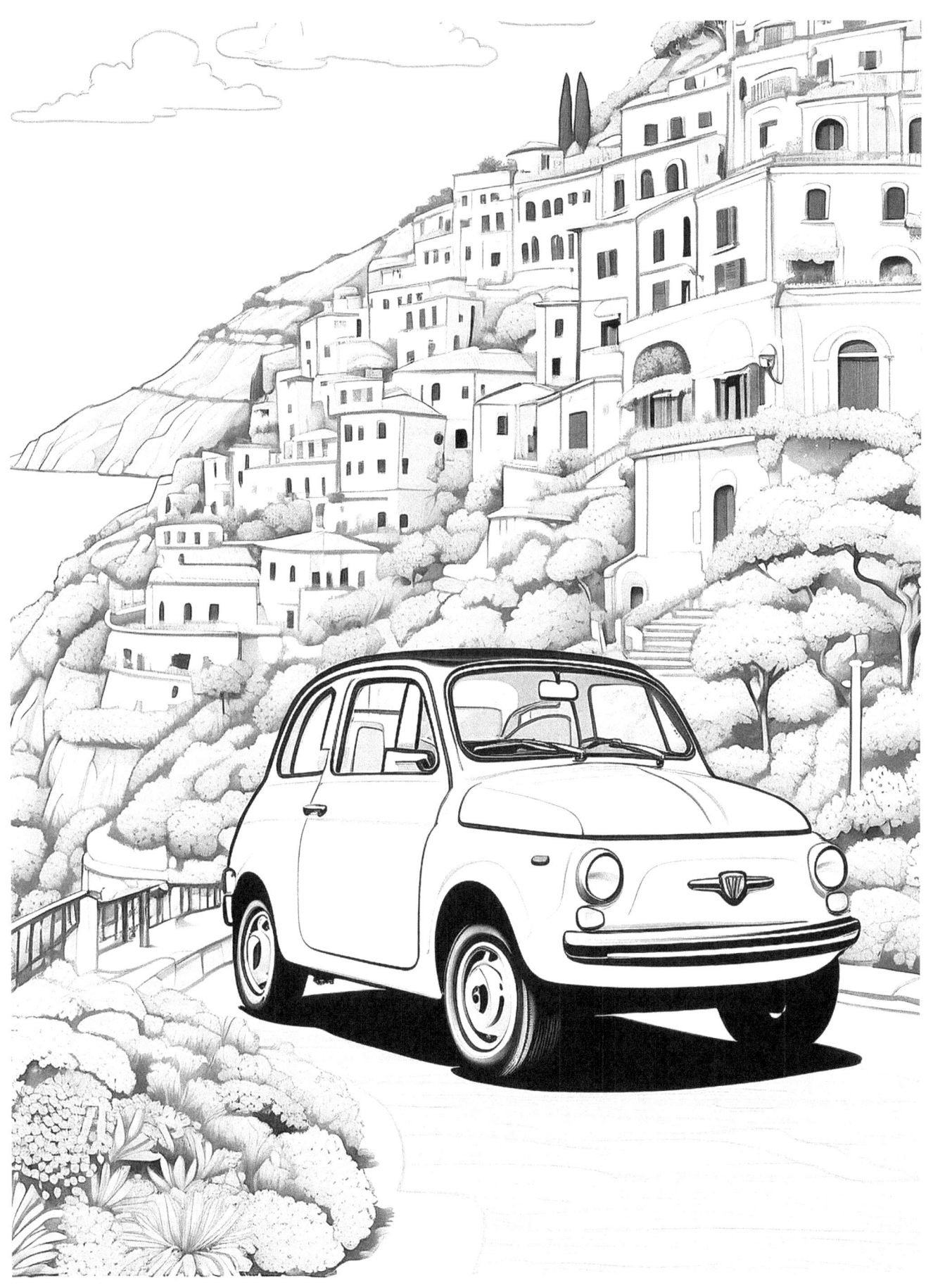

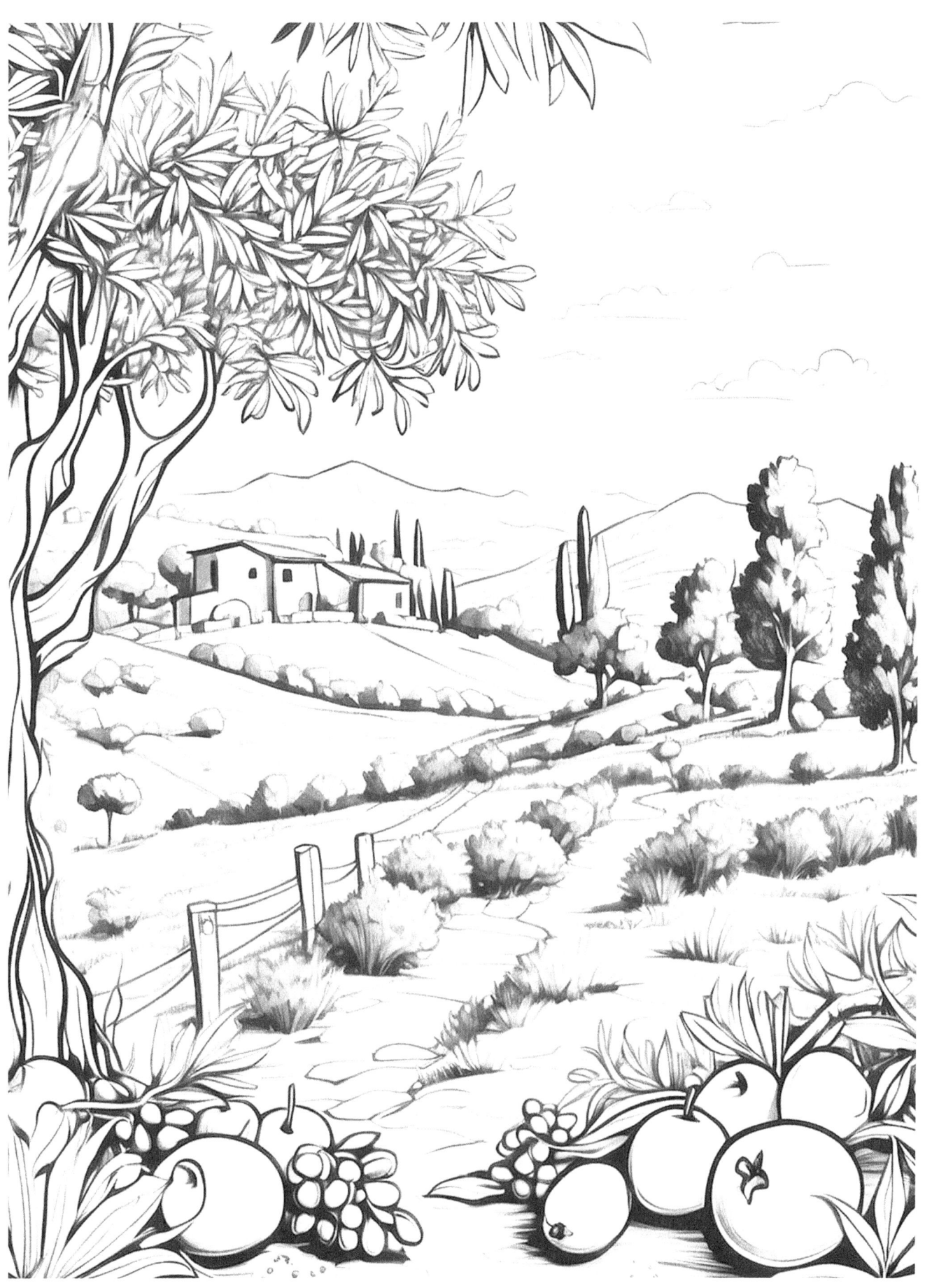

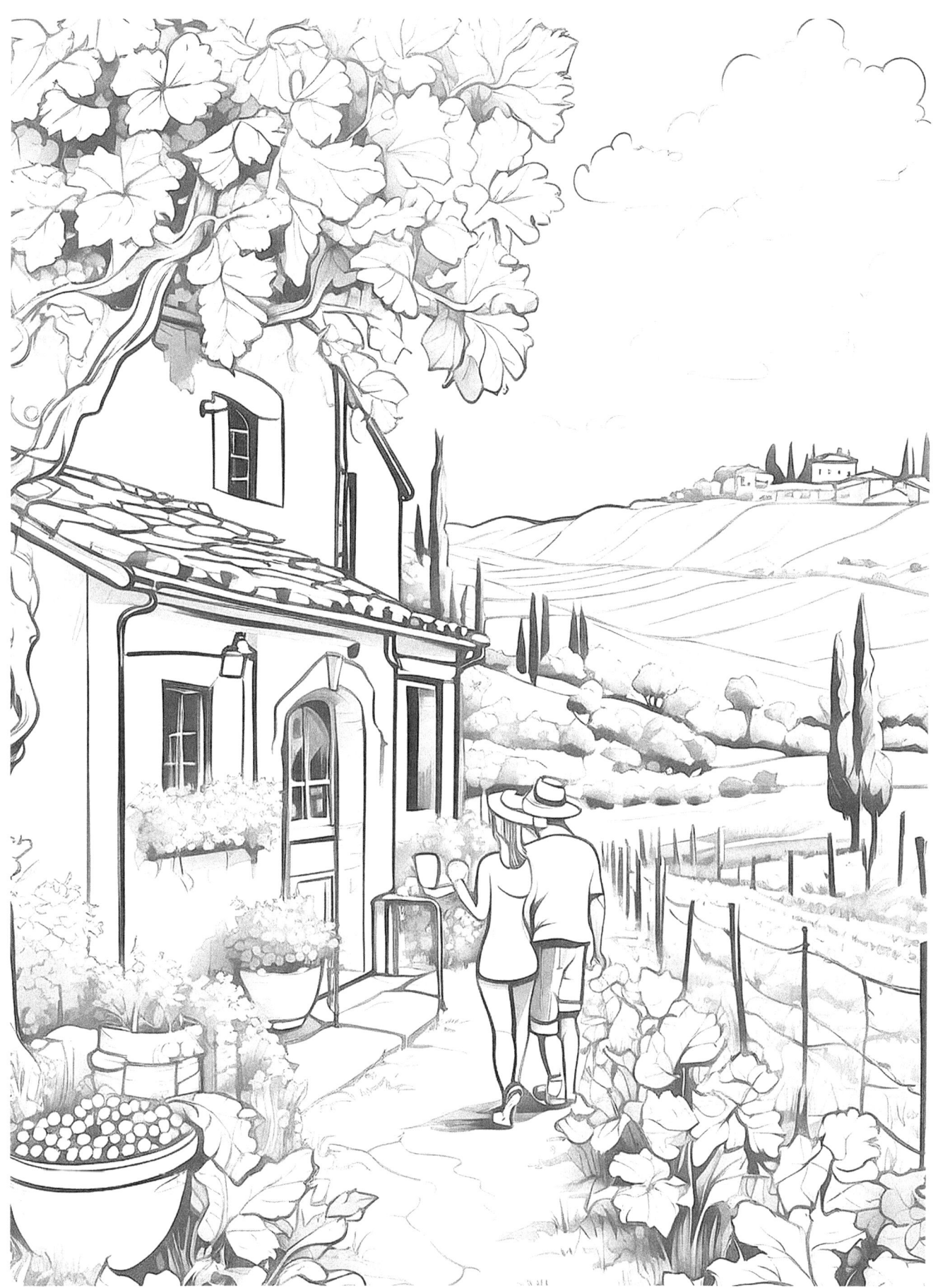

Dear Friends,
as we reach the end of this journey through the fascinating world of Italian summer, I want to express heartfelt gratitude for sharing this colorful adventure with me. It has been an honor to accompany you as the drawings came to life under your creative hands. Each stroke of color made this journey unique and extraordinary. Thank You for Your Dedication and Creativity! I invite you to continue the adventure in the magical world of colors. May every brushstroke or pencil line be an opportunity to explore new horizons and bring forth new stories. Your artistic journey does not end here. Be inspired, explore, and keep coloring the world with your unique creativity.